Noah Simmons

Heroes and Heroines of the Fort Dearborn Massacre

Noah Simmons

Heroes and Heroines of the Fort Dearborn Massacre

ISBN/EAN: 9783744724340

Printed in Europe, USA, Canada, Australia, Japan

Cover: Foto ©ninafisch / pixelio.de

More available books at **www.hansebooks.com**

HEROES AND HEROINES

OF THE

FORT DEARBORN MASSACRE.

—A—

ROMANTIC AND TRAGIC HISTORY

—OF—

CORPORAL JOHN SIMMONS AND HIS HEROIC WIFE,

—ALSO OF—

THE FIRST WHITE CHILD BORN IN CHICAGO. THE LAST SURVIVOR OF THE HORRID BUTCHERY. A FULL AND TRUE RECITAL OF MARVELOUS FORTITUDE, MATCHLESS COURAGE AND TERRIBLE SUFFERINGS DURING THE BATTLE, THE MARCH, AND IN CAPTIVITY.

By N. SIMMONS, M. D.

LAWRENCE, KANSAS:
JOURNAL PUBLISHING COMPANY,
1896.

PREFACE.

Much of the material for this narrative has been obtained from Mrs. Simmons, an eye witness, and from her daughter, who was her companion in captivity, and with whom she resided for many years. Many histories have been consulted, but they are most unsatisfactory in their treatment of the details of the Fort Dearborn massacre, while the only reference to John Simmons on file in the department at Washington is that he drew $60 for his first year's service as a soldier.

By the kind courtesy of E. G. Mason, Esq., President of the Chicago Historical Society, his masterly address, delivered at the unveiling of the Pullman Memorial Monument on the 22d of June, 1893, is inserted. In behalf of the large number of relatives and friends of the principal parties whose names are mentioned in this little book, I desire to express here their grateful acknowledgments to George M. Pullman, the donor of the beautiful monument to the memory of the slain of the massacre, and all associated with him in its conception and execution, especially E. G. Mason, historian, and Carl Rorhl-Smith, sculptor of the monument.

My apology for this intrusion into the already overwrought field of authorship is a desire to do justice to the memory of a brave soldier and his devoted wife, and also to add a few facts to the brief history of the Fort Dearborn massacre.

The heroines and heroes of that awful day, whose blood sank into the sand dunes by the lake, or who experienced in captivity, an even more dreadful fate, are almost forgotten, but it may be interesting to know that the butchers of Fort Dearborn and their descendents have annually received many thousands of dollars from the United States government for their support.

The name of the ancestors of John Simmons in Switzerland was Simons, the additional letter being first employed after their arrival in America.

CONTENTS.

PAGE.

PREFACE..3

CHAPTER I.
A FORTUNATE MEETING IN THE WILDERNESS.........9

CHAPTER II.
MARRIED AND ENLISTED..........................13

CHAPTER III.
THE STORM GATHERING...........................15

CHAPTER IV.
A TOUR THROUGH THE WILDERNESS.................20

CHAPTER V.
LIFE AT FORT DEARBORN.........................25

CHAPTER VI.
THE ORDER TO EVACUATE THE FORT................28

CHAPTER VII.
PREPARING TO EVACUATE THE FORT................31

CHAPTER VIII.
THE BATTLE AND MASSACRE.......................35

CHAPTER IX.
Captivity and Ransom..........................52

CHAPTER X.
The Massacre of Neighbors Her only Sister among Them........................61

CHAPTER XI.
At Rest...67

CHAPTER XII.
Awaiting the End...............................69

CHAPTER XIII.
The Pottawatomie Tribe.........................72

BLACK PARTRIDGE RETURNING HIS MEDAL.

N. SIMMONS, M. D.

HEROES AND HEROINES OF THE FORT DEARBORN MASSACRE.

CHAPTER I.

A FORTUNATE MEETING IN THE WILDERNESS.

One bright evening in the early springtime of 1801 two wagon trains entered simultaneously a beautiful grove on the banks of a limpid stream in eastern Ohio. The leaders of these trains at once discovered in each other friends and associates of boyhood days in the far away land of their nativity—charming Switzerland. In early manhood they had emigrated to America and without prearrangement become neighbors in Pennsylvania. Phillip Simmons with his wife and only son, John, had settled in York county on the Susquehanna river, while later on, the elder Millhouse located on the opposite shore of the same stream in Lancaster county. This opportune meeting in a strange land which both had sought for new homes was the welcome renewal of the former acquaintance in dear old Switzerland. This close relation of comradeship between the families continued for many years and was not fully dissolved until the year 1800, when Phillip Simmons and his wife having passed away in the ripened maturity of wholesome lives,

John Simmons was left at the head of the family, his own household consisting of six hardy sons and four daughters. To provide homes for this large family he determined to move to West Virginia. A short residence there convinced this descendent of Alpine mountains that he had not as yet found a satisfactory abiding place. The bold freeman resolved that his children should not live under the blighting influences of human slavery. This purpose led him to consider seriously the possibilities of obtaining homes on a soil free from the hated institution. Fortunately, at that time one of the grandest domains on earth had been recently dedicated to freedom.

The ordinance of 1787 forever prohibited slavery in the Northwest Territory lying north and west of the Ohio river. The resources of this new land were the subject of almost fabulous tales of its wonderful productiveness, the mildness of its climate, the beautiful streams fed by springs of crystal water, gurgling from the rocks and hill sides, the magnificent forests furnishing the finest timber for building purposes and teeming with wild game, the native grasses furnishing abundant food for horses and cattle, both winter and summer while the bountiful mast of the woods maintained the numerous hogs which ranged through them.

This mere outline of the reports reaching the older settlements through the soldiers returning from the campaigns of Harmer, St. Clair and Wayne had awakened the spirit of adventure in these home seekers to the extent that they determined to dare the dangers arising from the hostility of the savages and seek their fortunes in the new Territory of Ohio. Simultaneously the persons composing a train headed by Mr. Millhouse, had arrived at the same conclusion, hence the meeting in the wilderness. In the early morning following, the leaders of the two trains determined to cast their fortunes together on the remainder of the journey to the great Miami valley in western Ohio. This combination of forces enabled the train to present a somewhat formidable aspect as each male member carried a rifle on his shoulder or strapped to his back and a serviceable knife in his belt.

In the Simmons family, John Simmons, Jr., a lad of but twelve years of age was the favorite, while the youngest daughter, Susan Millhouse, was most tenderly regarded by the other party. Though their parents had been friends and acquaintances, first in Switzerland, then again in Pennsylvania, John and Susan first met in camp, as above described. They soon became fast friends and they are here introduced to the reader as the hero and heroine of this narative.

Though John Simmons was but a mere boy, he was tall, strong and alert beyond his years. With his trusty rifle he furnished his full quota of game for the combined train and performed regular guard duty besides. Indeed his general usefulness in camp and on the journey rendered him a favorite with all. His genial spirit and cheerful bearing was especially recognized by Susan Millhouse, who looked upon the young frontiersman as her ideal of the coming hero, and manifested her partiality for his presence by little acts of favoritism. These evidences of deep esteem for John from the innocent girl were noticed with chagrin and mortification by a young man who had lived in the Millhouse family for some time, and was now emigrating with them to their new home. Thomas Rodgers was a fine athletic young fellow, but quiet and earnest. It had been his dream to win the hand of the youngest daughter of the Millhouse family, and it was with forebodings of disappointment that he witnessed the growing friendship between John Simmons and his idol. He continued to discharge his duties faithfully however, and with the exception of a disposition to ramble alone in the forest, seemingly without special purpose, and to isolate himself from society generally, no indication of his feeling was manifest. "Tom," as he was familiarly called, remained with the party to the end of the journey and with the Millhouse family long after the marriage of their daughter. With this simple statement Tom will be dismissed for the present.

CHAPTER II.

MARRIED AND ENLISTED.

After months of weary journeying the travelers finally stood upon the shore of the great Miami river near the present city of Dayton. Few settlers had preceded them and the only evidence of advancing civilization were the few military trails that traversed the wilderness between the outposts and Indian agencies. After a time spent in exploring lands along the Miami and its tributaries in the vicinity of Troy and Dayton, John Simmons, Sr., selected six quarter sections of fertile land on upper Lost Creek, six miles east of Col. Johnson's Indian Agency on the site of the present Piqua. Having secured titles to these lands, the men who were to occupy them proceeded to build a large two-story double log house at a central point near a fine spring of ever flowing cold water. The walls were pierced with loop holes; barricades and other means of defense were provided and all trees and bushes within gun-shot distance of the blockhouse were removed. It was consequently deemed impossible for an enemy to approach without exposure to the fire of the riflemen within. Here the family resided and in times of extreme danger the neighbors collected. It is needless to say that when Mr. Millhouse settled near the Simmons blockhouse, John, Jr., and Susan were delighted. Perhaps the latter had reminded her father that there were six stalwart riflemen in the Simmons family, whose protection would be desirable in case of attack by the savages, and possibly her wishes were consulted in the selection of the homestead site.

Years passed amid constant dangers from the time the emigrants crossed the Ohio river. At that time John Simmons was but twelve years old. Young as he was he had been constantly on duty and every moment on the alert to prevent surprise by the Indians or wild beasts. It was not strange therefore that after eight years of this mode of life he embraced the first opportunity that presented after he had reached the age and strength required, to enlist in the regular army, some of the most important duties in which service having been learned in these individual experiences. In March, 1808, John Simmons, Jr., and Susan Millhouse were married and in the latter part of 1809 David Simmons was born. On the 14th of March, 1810, John Simmons enlisted in Captain Whistler's Company, First Regiment, United States Infantry, afterward commanded by Captain Nathan Heald, and was assigned to duty at Fort Dearborn on the site of the city of Chicago.

CHAPTER III.

THE STORM GATHERING.

A brief study of the relation existing between the whites and Indians at this time is indispensable to a complete understanding of the perils that confronted the border settlers. As early as 1788 a settlement was made at Marietta and another at Cincinnati. The Indians alarmed at these and other aggressions maintained a constant warfare on the border pioneers, often crossing the Ohio river into Pennsylvania, Virginia and Kentucky and robbing isolated settlers and returning to their villages in the interior. To stop these predatory incursions and bring the Indians to terms, General Harmer was sent with an army of 1400 men into the country of the hostiles. Late in the autumn of 1790 he reached and destroyed the towns of the Miami Indians on the ground now occupied by Fort Wayne. The complete loss of their habitations and possessions was a severe blow to the savages, and doubtless rendered them desperate. To complete the work of destruction Gen. Harmer divided his army into three detachments which were cut to pieces in detail by the Indians under Little Turtle and Captain Wells.

On November 3d, 1791, Gen. Arthur St. Clair with 1400 soldiers encamped at Fort Recovery, near the Ohio and Indiana state line. On the following morning at early dawn the savages made a furious attack upon the camp which resulted in fearful slaughter and disastrous route of the surprised whites. Closely pursued the remnant of the army fled to Fort Washington. These victories emboldened the exhilarated Indians to repeated depredations and acts of pillage and murder. In August, 1794, Gen. Wayne, with 3000 troops attacked the hostiles near the Maumee Rapids and defeated them with great slaughter. Captain Wells, the former ally and son-in-law of Little Turtle acted as captain of scouts to Gen. Wayne. "Mad Anthony" took no trivial revenge upon the defeated enemy. Their fields and villages for fifty miles around were destroyed. Completely humbled and impoverished the late defiant victors sued for peace. Accordingly in 1795 a treaty was signed between Gen. Wayne and many of the Indian chiefs. A number refused to recognize the treaty however, and at once began to prepare for the continuation of hostilities. It was during this enforced peace, late in 1801 that the Simmons settlement was located in the interior of western Ohio in the midst of Indian villages. After Wayne's treaty a chain of forts was established on the border extending from Cincinnati west to Vincennes and St. Louis, north to Greenville, Fort Recovery, Fort Wayne, Fort Defiance, Fort Meigs, Detroit, Macinac, and northwest to Fort Dearborn (Chicago). Within this chain of posts were scores of Indian villages, teeming with old, scarred warriors who delighted in detailing the wrongs the tribes had suffered at the hands of the whites. The young warriors listened intently to these tales, and burned to avenge these indignities and injuries without delay. A leader alone was required to begin hostilities at once, and with the demand came the man. The leading chiefs of the powerful Shawnee tribe were Tecumseh and his twin brother Telskwatawa, known as "The Prophet," two eloquent orators and able leaders. Tecumseh stirred the young warriors to the verge of frenzy with his firey recital of the outrages inflicted upon the Indians by the whites, while the Prophet aroused the strong religious and superstitious feelings of the tribe by his mysterious incantations.

In 1806 Tecumseh and the Prophet established a village at Fort Greenville, twenty-six miles distant from the Simmons settlement, but in 1808 they removed to Tippecanoe, Indiana, to the great delight of the Ohio settlers. Undoubtedly this removal was made preparatory to the storm they intended should break upon the white settlers of the border, being for the purpose of placing their women and children beyond the doomed region.

In 1809 the apprehension of the whites reached its climax, and rapid preparations were made for defence. Block houses, often surrounded with stockades, were erected in each settlement. Militia companies were organized, and the whole population of the border put upon a war footing. In 1810, house burning, horse stealing and murders were daily on the increase and had become so common that Gen. Harrison sent a message to Tecumseh, declaring that if these crimes against the white settlers did not cease he might expect to be attacked. To this message Tecumseh replied in person, but the interview was stormy and unsatisfactory, and each proceeded at once to prepare for open hostilities; Tecumseh by visiting the Indian tribes in the south to secure their co-operation in the coming struggle, while Gen. Harrison collected his forces, and at once marched against the Shawnee village of Tippecanoe, where, on the 7th of November, 1811, he defeated the Indians after a desperate engagement, and destroyed the village with the accumulated provisions for the coming winter. The records of history afford no grander episode than that of the crusade of Tecumseh. This eloquent champion, stealthy as the panther of his native wilds sprang from one tribe to another and enkindled everywhere the smouldering embers of rapine and revenge into the fierce fires of war. But one theme was discussed at the numerous council fires which blazed from the oak forests of Michigan to the moss covered pines of Alabama. The whites were to be exterminated or driven across the Ohio. Many of the settlers had secured homes that were as dear to them as the lands on which they stood were to the Indians. So, to both parties it was to be a battle for their homes, therefore a battle to the death.

With the certainty of an Indian war and of a conflict with Great Britain it was evident that the recruits who enlisted in the American army in 1810 might confidently expect a speedy participation in bloody conflict. Against this assurance of the dangers of battle the government had only the paltry pittance of five dollars a month to offer these enlisted men, but the courage and patriotism that accepted these odds finds no worthy parallel. Grand as were all these voluntary supporters of the country in this dark hour, none were more sublime in sacrifice than Private John Simmons. A young and affectionate wife and a babe less than a year old were left behind while he went to engage in a war with fiendish savages who took no prisoners but to torture them to death in the most cruel manner. The only exceptions to this awful custom was furnished when a captive woman or child was occasionally spared with intent to impress as a slave or adopt by a warrior. From such an enemy no mercy need be expected. The result of each encounter was to be complete victory or dreadful death. It is difficult therefore for the men of this generation with its protracted season of peace and the almost universally acknowledged amenities of warfare to realize the value of such sacrifice and service.

CHAPTER IV.

A TOUR THROUGH THE WILDERNESS.

John Simmons reached Fort Dearborn early in the spring of 1810 and at once entered upon his military duties which he performed with skill and fidelity, and at the end of the first year of service he modestly received his promotion to corporal, and with it a furlough which enabled him to visit his family. He had often accompanied hunting and scouting parties along the lake shore and the Chicago river. He became enamored of the country around Fort Dearborn which is now occupied by Chicago and its suburbs. Swarms of water fowl covered the lakes and rivers while their waters teemed with the finest fish. Buffalo, elk, bear and deer, with a good variety of smaller game were found in abundance.

On the vast prairies and along the wooded river bottoms the tall grass attested the great fertility of the soil, while the ease with which a farm could be opened by merely plowing the prairie as compared with the task of clearing the timber lands of western Ohio and eastern Indiana induced the young soldier to determine to settle there at the expiration of his term of service. He believed and frequently expressed the conviction that a great city would eventually be built near the fort. It was with these anticipations that John Simmons left the garrison and with rapid strides traversed the intervening wilderness to his home in Miami county, Ohio. Looking back almost a century one can scarcely realize the extasy with which the returned soldier met his aged father and mother, his devoted wife and curly headed boy who had in his absence taken his first steps, and learned to pronounce the sacred words "Mama" and "Papa." Equally difficult would it be for us to understand the emotions of the individual members of the little household as the stalwart young officer, from whom presumably nothing had been heard during his absence, passed the heavy door and entered the well guarded enclusure.

As John Simmons unfolded the marvelous tales of the Illinois country all members of the rejoicing family listened with engrossed interest. The vast meadows covered with luxuriant grass waving in the breeze, and bounded only to the observers view by the horizon, the herds of buffalo, deer and elk pasturing on these prairies, furnishing an abundance of excellent meat, while the lakes and rivers swarmed with an inexhaustible supply of food. His enthusiastic description produced unbounded admiration and the narrator improved the advantage he had gained by revealing his desire to make the delectable land his future home, and for that purpose to take his little family with him on his return. This proposition startled his aged parents who having emigrated from Europe to Pennsylvania, thence to Ohio, shrank from the thought of removing to Illinois. But the arguments John employed were so reasonable that they interposed but feeble opposition and contented themselves by expressing regrets that the parting must so soon occur and the hope that at the expiration of his term of service he would return to them and make his home on the land which they had given him. To Mrs. Simmons, Jr., the return with her husband to Fort Dearborn was a momentous matter. It involved a journey of four hundred miles through an almost trackless wilderness on foot with no shelter save that afforded by a small canvass stretched over the boughs of trees. But she had learned to trust her young soldier husband implicitly and for admirable cause. They had journeyed together from eastern Ohio to their home in Miami county, as neighbors and lovers they had been intimately acquainted for seven years; she had scarcely claimed him as her own before surrendering him to her country as a soldier. His promotion in the absence of wealth or influential friends to urge his cause was to her the best assurance of his merit. As he stood before her, nearly six feet in height, with massive frame, in the liberal endowment of muscular young manhood, clad in the neat army uniform, a mature man, an experienced backwoodsman and a brave soldier, his young wife felt that his plea for her companionship during the remaining period of his enlistment was already granted. Never had his influence over her been so controling, her love for him so overpowering. It was, however, no blind passion which assented to the hard conditions of the proposition. The devoted wife was no novice in the knowledge of the dangers to be expected on the contemplated journey. It was therefore with full understanding of the situation that she gave her cheerful consent to accompany her husband on his return.

Mrs. Simmons, although of but medium height, possessed a physical frame and organization capable of great endurance. Aware, at least partially, of the demands to be made upon her constitution, she entered into the work of preparation for the journey intelligently, and the progress of the dreary march revealed her wise forethought in providing as far as possible for the comfort and relief of her cherished companions. Still, little time remained to complete the preparations and little was the amount they were able to transport, as a single pack horse was expected to carry the cooking utensils, camp equipage, provisions and extra clothing. John led the horse and bore his heavy rifle upon which so much of the safety and supply of the little party depended, while Susan trudged along carrying the child. So they set out one morning in the latter part of March, 1811. The last parting had been a trying event. To the friends who had collected to see the adventurous pilgrims depart on their fearful journey it seemed the last farewell. To the aged father and mother of both John and Susan the parting was indescribably painful. Little David received a full share of tearful affection of all who had known him as the sunshine of the home he had so recently come to bless, and which was to see him no more. Reasonable as were the sad anticipations of the sorrowful friends, none could foretell the awful fate of the small party, but one of whom was to return.

On the first day the family was escorted to Piqua where they crossed the Miami river and pushed on to Stillwater, where Covington now stands and there encamped, having traveled fifteen miles. On the second day they reached Fort Greenville. Here their escort returned. From Fort Greenville they bore a little west of north to Fort Recovery, a distance of thirty-five miles. Their next point was Fort Wayne, distance eighty miles, where they rested for a day and secured provisions for the remainder of the journey to Fort Dearborn, the route traveled being near two hundred miles. The time occupied in making the trip to Fort Dearborn from Ohio was about thirty days. To persons acquainted with the country traveled it is a marvel that they succeeded in making the journey in that time, as at that season of the year (April) the streams were usually full and difficult to ford, and they were compelled to make long detours to pass around the swamps covered with water which lay on their way. Then, the constant fear of falling in with scalping parties of savages required incessant watchfulness. Wearisome days were succeeded by sleepless nights and neither of the parents for an hour were free from apprehension.

Long years after this journey, while Mrs. Simmons enjoyed repose in the society of friends she often declared that she enjoyed the trip as though it had been a pleasure excursion, but it is possible that this view was suggested by the contrast with her subsequent experiences.

CHAPTER V.

LIFE AT FORT DEARBORN.

It was late in April when the little party entered the gate at Fort Dearborn, tired and foot sore. The young soldier was complimented by his comrades in arms for his bravery in making the journey to and from Ohio. A universal favorite before, this adventure greatly enhanced his reputation as a soldier of skill and spirit. His superior officers confided important duties to his care and command which he always executed with the strictest fidelity. Mrs. Simmons watched with admiration and delight the growing confidence reposed in her husband. For herself, she soon shared with her husband the esteem of the entire garrison.

The people of the fort, consisting of soldiers, women and children, were less than one hundred in number. The imminence of a common danger united all in a common union. They were far from civilization, far from succor in case of an attack by a strong enemy. Rumors of threatened hostilities were frequently brought to the fort by scouts or friendly Indians. Into such a community, thus bound together by a tie stronger than any known to humanity, it was not difficult for the heroic woman to obtain speedy entrance into any circle in the limited society of the post. Her splendid courage and endurance during the long and wearisome march, and her thorough acquaintance with Indian character, acquired by long residences in the midst of savage settlements, rendered her opinions almost as valuable as those of her husband. On account of his participation in the journey, little David, now three years old, was familiarly called "the little curly headed corporal," and soon became a pet of all in the garrison.

In November, 1811, Gen. Harrison defeated the Indians at Tippecanoe and destroyed their village. The loss to the hostiles of the stores collected for winter entailed great hardship upon them. The news of this battle reached Fort Dearborn by the way of Detroit, Fort Macinac and lake Michigan, and warned the garrison of impending danger. The gratification over the success of the engagement was mingled in the minds of the occupants of the isolated post by the reflection that while it was then too late in the season for the enraged tribes to lay siege to Fort Dearborn a renewal of hostilities might be expected on the return of spring.

Aggressions and indignities were so frequently inflicted upon American citizens by the officers and agents of the English government, that in June, 1812, war was declared against Great Britain, and in July the British and Indians captured Fort Macinac. The officers of this post first learned of the declaration of war from the enemy, a fact which suggests incompetency or criminal neglect on the part of high officials.

On the 12th day of February, 1812, a daughter was born to Corporal Simmons, being one of the first white children, if not the first, born within the limits of the present city of Chicago. She came to brighten the few remaining months of her little brother's life, as a source of consolation to her mother in widowhood and bondage, and to sustain and comfort her in her declining years. At this writing she is reposing at the age of 83 years in the beautiful California home of her daughter. In honor of his devoted wife, Corporal Simmons named the little stranger Susan Simmons.

CHAPTER VI.

THE ORDER TO EVACUATE THE FORT.

With Macinac, the key to lake Michigan, in possession of the British and Indians, with Detroit practically beleaguered, while assistance from Fort Wayne or Vincennes was out of the question, Fort Dearborn should have been evacuated at once. There were no settlers near to protect, the garrison was too weak to venture beyond the walls of the fort and too far from other military posts to render them any assistance or to receive succor from them in case of attack. Such was the condition of Fort Dearborn on the seventh day of August, 1812, when Captain Heald received the order from Gen. Hull, who had reported to the war department on July 29th, that he would send "at once." The order being nine days in transit reached the fort on the 7th of August. It was obvious that every moment of delay increased the danger of the garrison. Whether it should be decided to remain or withdraw, this fact was equally manifest. Why, therefore, Captain Heald faltered for seven days is a serious question. The inexplicable delay gave the Indians an opportunity to collect their warriors from the Pottawatomie villages in the vicinity. This was done industriously during the week extending from the 7th to the 14th of August.

On the 14th of August Captain Heald determined to evacuate the fort on the following day. On that day he concluded a treaty with the Indians by the terms of which the savages were to be given all the stores of the fort not required on the march in consideration of which the Indians stipulated to escort the garrison to Fort Wayne in safety. On the evening of the 14th, after the treaty had been made and the Indians had doubtless fully matured their plans for the following day, which without doubt included the capture of the entire garrison when decoyed into the open prairie, Black Partridge, a Pottawatomie chief, warned Captain Heald of the determination on the part of the Indians by returning to him a valuable medal with the statement that his young men had determined to wash their hands in the blood of the whites and that he could not restrain them. Then, in tones of sadness, he closed his remarkable speech with the most emphatic warning, saying: "Linden birds have been singing in my ears to-day; be careful on the march you are about to make." The fact that near five hundred armed warriors had collected in the immediate vicinity of the fort of itself boded no good to the garrison, but the warning of Black Partridge, couched in the most significant language and delivered in terms of sadness and sorrow, should have changed doubt and suspicion in the mind of Captain Heald into positive certainty. Perhaps the warning came too late for the commandant to retrace his steps and prepare for defense, but it should have led to more prudent alignment of the troops on the line of retreat. The destruction of surplus stores, notably powder and whiskey, while perhaps justifiable on account of the inevitable excesses their possession would cause, was made a pretext by the Indians to excuse their treachery. But the falseness of this plea is proved by the words of Black Partridge, which shows that the bloody purpose had been determined on before the evacuation. Still, it may be possible that the act stimulated the savages to greater cruelty in their treatment of the whites. If there was any doubt as to the good intentions of Black Partridge in warning the garrison on the evening before the evacuation, it disappeared as the fact of his repeated intervention to save the lives of the doomed inmates was manifest

It was a rash and ill considered act on the part of the government in planting a feeble post so far from support. Immediately upon the declaration of war, and especially after the fall of Mackinac it should have been evacuated. Promptly on the receipt of Gen. Hull's discretionary order Captain Heald should have abandoned the fort, and marched with all possible speed to Fort Wayne or he should have made the best possible preparation for defense and seige, but seven days of indecision coupled with previous neglect and incompetency caused the destruction of the brave garrison and the obliteration of the first Chicago.

CHAPTER VII.

PREPARING TO EVACUATE THE FORT.

On the evening of the 14th the garrison was busy loading the wagons for the journey which would occupy from eight to ten days. Provisions and camp equipage constituted the principal part of these loads. In the grave peril which confronted them the members of the garrison were more united in sentiment and action than ever before. The soldiers filled their powder horns, adjusted their flints, loaded their bullet pouches, and every possible preparation was made for defense, believing the moment they left the friendly walls of the fort they would be at the mercy of an overwhelming army of savages. Many of the little Spartan band vowed to defend the women and children with their lives, and for this purpose the best possible preparations were made. Corporal Simmons fully realized the fearful responsibility that rested upon him, and not one of the small command prepared to march through the gate of the fort and out into the presence of the Indians with a firmer determination to do his whole duty. True not one of them had greater incentive to perform a soldier's part. His constant thought was of the noble woman who had been his faithful friend on the perilous journey through the wilderness of Ohio, and later became his idolized wife; and who in a spirit fitting a soldier's bride, gave him to the service of his country a little more than two years before. His heart swelled often while engaged in the monotonous routine of his regular duty as he recalled her grand comradeship, on the long tramp through the dense forests in western Ohio and across Indiana to this forlorn hope. Intimately and inseparably connected with remembrances of his heroic wife, Corporal Simmons never forgot their first born, little David, the "curly headed corporal," full of life and happy in the love of papa and mama, and the infant Susan, six months and two days old, the delight and joy of the little family and the pet and play fellow of even the roughest soldiers in the camp. On that sad evening, as John Simmons looked upon this group confided to his protection he resolved that harm could only reach them over his dead body. With what fidelity he redeemed this vow will be revealed later on.

The great number of warriors camped in the immediate vicinity of the fort required a strong guard for the night to prevent a surprise. The other soldiers slept a fitful sleep upon their arms. The women of the garrison, a majority of whom had small children, were busy in preparing for the march. Among these was Mrs. Simmons, who early in the evening had endeavored to put her babe to sleep so that she might complete the preparations necessary for the long march. The "little corporal," David, had noticed the unusual stir and preparation going on around him, and was exceedingly anxious to know what it all meant. "Where were they going?" "Would he ride in the big wagon?" "Were they going to grandpa's in Ohio?" These with many other questions were eagerly asked and years afterward rang in the ears of Mrs. Simmons when she recalled the events of that last gloomy night in Fort Dearborn. It was late in the evening when little David, tired of watching the busy scene and overcome by weariness, repeated his little prayer on his mother's lap for the last time and received his good night kiss from father and mother. The young soldier and wife now discussed the probabilities of the morrow. He was familiar with all the details of the proposed evacuation. During the day Captain Wells one of the most famous Indian fighters of the frontier arrived with twenty friendly warriors of the Miami tribe, for the purpose of rendering assistance to the beleaguered garrison or to escort them to Fort Wayne in case of evacuation. Captain Wells was present and heard the declaration of Black Partridge that his young men had determined to imbue their hands in the blood of the whites and that he could not restrain them. Wells knew the chief intimately and reposed the utmost confidence in his truthfulness. This statement therefore convinced him of the danger which confronted them. Corporal Simmons informed his wife of the order to secretly destroy the whiskey and ammunition which Captain Heald had promised the Indians, and of his belief that should the savages discover this they would not hesitate to murder the garrison. He did not conceal from her his opinion that the peril seemed imminent for he realized that the whites would be compelled to fight for their lives with odds of eight to one against them. It may be well supposed that the night was far advanced before sleep came to their relief from the heavy burdens which oppressed mind and body, and that early dawn found them astir and preparing for the fearful ordeal before them. All night dark objects were seen moving about outside the fort, showing to the guards who were ever on the alert that the Indians were on the watch to prevent the admittance of farther reinforcements and the dispatch of couriers for succor.

At an early hour on the morning of the 15th day of August, 1812, the troops were mustered within the stockade and inspected. The roll was called and answered for the last time. Fifty-four regular soldiers and twelve militia men stood in line, presenting a feeble array with which to engage five hundred fierce warriors on the open prairie. The troops were dismissed for the last breakfast they were destined to eat together, with orders to be ready to march at nine o'clock. While the troops were engaged in eating breakfast and preparing for the march the Indians just outside the stockade were eating a meal furnished from the stores of the fort the day before, and arranging apparently to escort the garrison on its march to safety, while in reality they were preparing to decoy it to its doom.

CHAPTER VIII.

THE BATTLE AND MASSACRE.

Preparations for the evacuation having been completed and the fatal hour having arrived, the line of march was formed within the stockade as described by E. G. Mason, Esq., President of the Chicago Historical Society, in his masterly address delivered at the unveiling of the Pullman Memorial Monument, which is here inserted in full, as follows:

"The Chicago Historical Society accepts this noble gift in trust for our city and for posterity with high appreciation of the generosity, the public spirit, and the regard for history of the donor. It realizes that this monument so wisely planned and so superbly executed is to be preserved not simply as a splendid ornament of our city but also as a most impressive record of its history. This group, representing to the life the thrilling scene enacted perchance on the very spot on which it stands, barely eighty years ago, and its present surroundings, make most vivid the tremendous contrast between the Chicago of 1812 and the Chicago of 1893. It teaches thus the marvelous growth of our city, and it commemorates as well the trials and the sorrows of those who suffered here in the cause of civilization. The tragedy which it recalls, though it seemed to extinguish the infant settlement in blood, was in reality one which nerved men's arms and fired their hearts to the efforts which rescued this region from the invader and the barbarian. The story which it tells is therefore of deeper significance than many that have to do with

> 'Battles, and the breath
> Of stormy war and violent death,'

and it is one which should never be forgotten.

"With its suggestions before us how readily we can picture to ourselves the events of that 15th day of August in the year of grace 1812. Hardly a week before there had come through the forest and across the prairie to the lonely Fort Dearborn an Indian runner, like a clansman with the fiery cross, bearing the news of the battle and disaster. War with Great Britain had been declared in June, Mackinac had fallen into the hands of the enemy in July, and with these alarming tidings the red messenger brought an order from the commanding general at Detroit, contemplating the abandonment of this frontier post. Concerning the terms of his order authorities have differed. Capt. Heald, who received it, speaks of it as a peremptory command to evacuate the fort. Others with good means of knowledge say that the dispatch directed him to vacate the fort if practicable. But General Hull who sent the order, settles this question in a report to the War Department which has recently come to light. Writing under date of July 29th, 1812, he says:

"'I shall immediately send an express to Fort Dearborn with orders to evacuate that post and retreat to this place (Detroit) or Fort Wayne, provided it can be effected with a greater prospect of safety than to remain. Capt. Heald is a judicious officer and I shall confide much to his discretion.'

"The decision whether to go or stay rested therefore with Capt. Nathan Heald, and truly the responsibility was a heavy one. Signs of Indian hostility had not been wanting. But the evening before Black Partridge, a chief of the Pottawatomie tribe, long a friend of the whites, had entered the quarters of the commanding officer and handed to him the medal which the warrior wore in token of services to the American cause in the Indian campaigns of 'Mad' Anthony Wayne. With dignity and with sadness the native orator said:

"'Father, I come to deliver up to you the medal I wear. It was given me by the Americans, and I have long worn it in token of our mutual friendship. But our young men are resolved to imbue their hands in the blood of the whites. I cannot restrain them and I will not wear a token of peace while I am compelled to act as an enemy.'

"This striking incident has been fitly chosen as the subject of one of the reliefs on the pedestal of the monument. It typifies the relations between the hapless whites and their red neighbors at the moment and the causes which had changed friendship into hatred, and it sounds the note of coming doom.

"On that dreary day one gleam of light fell across the path of the perplexed commander. Capt. William Wells arrived from Fort Wayne with a small party of friendly Miami Indians to share the fortunes of the imperiled garrison. This gallant man, destined to be the chief hero and victim of the Chicago massacre, had had a most remarkable career. Of a good Kentucky family, he was stolen when a boy of 12 by the Miami Indians and adopted by their great chief, Me-che-kau-nah-qua, or Little Turtle, whose daughter became his wife. He fought on the side of the red men in their defeat of Gen Harmar in 1790 and Gen. St. Clair in 1791. Discovered by his Kentucky kindred when he had reached years of manhood, he was persuaded to ally himself with his own race, and took formal leave of his Indian comrades, avowing henceforth his enmity to them. Joining

Wayne's army, he was made captain of a company of scouts, and was a most faithful and valuable officer. When peace came with the treaty of Greenville in 1795, he devoted himself to obtaining an education, and succeeded so well that he was appointed Indian agent and served in that capacity at Chicago as early as 1803, and later at Fort Wayne, where he was also government interpreter and a Justice of the Peace. Here he heard of the probable evacuation of the post at Chicago, and knowing the temper of the Indians, he gathered such force as he could and made a rapid march across the country to save or die with his friends at Fort Dearborn, among whom the wife of Capt. Heald was his own favorite niece, whose gentle influence had been most potent in winning him back from barbarism years before. It seemed almost as if he had resolved to atone for the period in which he had ignorantly antagonized his own people by a supreme effort in their behalf against the race which had so nearly made him a savage.

"He came too late to effect any change in Capt. Heald's plans. The abandonment was resolved upon, and the stores and ammunition were in part destroyed and in part divided among the Indians, who were soon to make so base a return for these gifts. At 9 o'clock on that fatal summer morning the march began from the little fort, which stood where Michigan avenue and River street now join on a slight eminence around which the river wound to find its way to the lake near the present terminus of Madison street. The garrison bade farewell to the rude stockade and the log barracks and magazine and two corner blockhouses which composed the first Fort Dearborn. · When this only place of safety was left behind, the straggling line stretched out along the shore of the lake, Capt. Wells and a part of his Miamis in the van, half a company of regulars and a dozen militiamen, and the wagons with the women and children following, and the remainder of the Miamis bringing up the rear. You may see it all on the panel on the monument, which recalls from the past and makes very real this mournful march to death. The escort of Pottawatomies, which that treacherous tribe had glibly promised to Capt. Heald, kept abreast of the troops until they reached the sand hills intervening between the prairie and the lake, and here the Indians disappeared behind the ridge. The whites kept on near the water to a point a mile and a half from the fort and about where Fourteenth street now ends, when Wells in the advance was seen to turn and ride back, swinging his hat around his head in a circle, which meant in the sign language of the frontier: 'We are surrounded by Indians.'

"As soon as he came within hearing he shouted: 'We are surrounded; march up on the sand ridges.' And all at once, in the graphic language of Mrs. Heald, they saw 'the Indians' heads sticking up and down again, here and there, like turtles out of the water.'

"Instantly a volley was showered down from the sand hills, the troops were brought into line, and charged up the bank, one man, a veteran of seventy years, falling as they ascended. Wells shouted to Heald, 'Charge them!' and then led on and broke the line of the Indians, who scattered right and left. Another charge was made, in which Wells did deadly execution upon the perfidious barbarians, loading and firing two pistols and a gun in rapid succession. But the Pottawatomies, beaten in front, closed in on the flanks. The cowardly Miamis rendered no assistance, and in fifteen minutes' time the savages had possession of the baggage train and were slaying the women and children. Heald and the remnant of his command were isolated on a mound in the prairie. He had lost all his officers and half his men, was himself sorely wounded, and there was no choice but to surrender.

"Such, in merest outline, was the battle, and one of its saddest incidents was the death of Capt. Wells. As he rode back from the fray, desperately wounded, he met his niece and bade her farewell, saying: 'Tell my wife, if you live to see her—but I think it doubtful if a single one escapes—tell her I died at my post; doing the best I could. There are seven red devils over there that I have killed.' As he spoke his horse fell, pinning him to the ground. A group of Indians approached; he took deliberate aim and fired, killing one of them. As the others drew near, with a last effort he proudly lifted his head, saying: 'Shoot away,' and the fatal shot was fired.

"So died Chicago's hero, whose tragic fate and the hot fight in which he fell are aptly selected as the subjects of the other bas-reliefs of this monument. The bronze group which crowns it is an epitome of the whole struggle, revealing its desperate character, the kind of foemen whom our soldiers had to meet, and their mode of warfare, their merciless treatment of women and children, and setting forth the one touch of romance in the grim record of the Chicago massacre. It illustrates the moment when the young wife of Lieut. Helm, second in command of the fort, was attacked by an Indian lad, who struck her on the shoulder with a tomahawk. To prevent him from using his weapons she siezed him around the neck and strove to get possession of the scalping-knife which hung in a scabbard over his breast. In the midst of the struggle she was dragged from the grasp of her assailant by an older Indian. He bore her to the lake and plunged her into the waves; but she quickly perceived that his object was not to drown her, as he held her head above water. Gazing intently at him she soon recognized, in spite of the paint with which he was disguised, the whilom friend of the whites, Black Partridge, who saved her from further harm and restored her to her friends. For this good deed, and others, too, this noble chief should be held in kindly remembrance.

"It is difficult to realize that such scenes could have taken place where we meet to-day; but history and tradition alike bear witness that we are assembled near the center of that bloody battlefield. From the place on the lake shore a few blocks to the north, where Wells' signal halted the column over the parallel sand ridges southwesterly along the prairie and through the bushy ravines between, the running fight continued probably as far as the present intersection of Twenty-first street and Indiana avenue, where one of our soldiers was slain and scalped, and still lies buried. Just over on Michigan avenue must have been the little eminence on the prairie on which Heald made his last rally, and right before us the skulking savages, who had given away at the advance of our men, gathered in their rear around the few wagons which had vainly sought to keep under the cover of our line.

"If this gaunt old cottonwood, long known as the 'Massacre Tree,' could speak, what a tale of horror it would tell. For tradition, strong as Holy Writ, affirms that between this tree and its neighbor, the roots of which still remain beneath the pavement, the baggage wagon containing twelve children of the white families of the fort, and one young savage climbed into it, tomahawked the entire group.* A little while and this sole witness of that deed of woe must pass away. But the duty of preserving

---

*Mrs. Simmons was perhaps the only person who witnessed the details in and around the government wagon who escaped from captivity, and she always placed the number of children killed in the wagon at nine, the other three who were murdered were on foot.

the name and the locality of the Chicago massacre, which has been its charge for so many years, is now transferred to this stately monument, which will faithfully perform it long after the fall of the 'Massacre Tree.'

"Capt. Heald's whole party, not including the Miami detachment, when they marched out of Fort Dearborn comprised fifty-four regulars, twelve militiamen, nine women and eighteen children—ninety-three white persons in all. Of these twenty-six regulars and the twelve militiamen were slain in action, two women and twelve children were murdered on the field, and five regulars were barbarously put to death, after the surrender. There remained then but thirty-six of the whole party of ninety-three, and of the sixty-six fighting men who met their red foemen here that day only twenty-three survived. These, with seven women and six children, were prisoners in the hands of the savages. We know of the romantic escape, by the aid of friendly Indians, of Capt. and Mrs. Heald and Lieut. and Mrs. Helm; and three of the soldiers, one of whom was Orderly Sergeant William Griffith, in less than two months after the massacre found their way to Michigan, bringing the sad news from Fort Dearborn. Hull's surrender had placed Detroit in the hands of the enemy; but the Territorial Chief Justice, Woodward, the highest United States authority there, in a ringing letter to the British Commander, Col. Proctor, under date of October 8, 1812, demanded in the name of humanity that instant means should be taken for the preservation of these unhappy captives by sending special messengers among the Indians to collect the prisoners and bring them to the nearest army post, and that orders to co-operate should be issued to the British officers on the lakes. Col. Proctor one month before had been informed by his own people of the bloody work at Chicago, and had reported the same to his superior offcer, Maj. Gen. Brock, but had contented himself with remarking that he had no knowledge of any attack having been intended by the Indians on Chicago, nor could they indeed be said to be within the influence of the British.

"Now, spurred to action by Judge Woodward's clear and forcible presentation of the case, Proctor promised to use the most effective means in his power for the speedy release from slavery of these unfortunate individuals. He committed the matter to Robert Dickson, British agent to the Indians of the Western Nations, who proceeded about it leisurely enough. March 16, 1813, he wrote from St. Joseph's Lake, Michigan, that there remained of the ill-fated garrison of Chicago, captives among the Indians, seventeen soldiers, four women, and some children, and that he had taken the necessary steps for their redemption and had the fullest confidence that he should succeed in getting the whole. Six days later he came to Chicago and inspected the ruined fort, where, as he says, there remained only two pieces of brass ordinance, three-pounders—one in the river, with wheels, and the other dismounted—a powder magazine, well preserved, and a few houses on the outside of the fort, in good condition. The desolation apparently was not relieved by the presence of a single inhabitant. Such was the appearance of Chicago in the spring following the massacre. Of these seventeen soldiers, the nine who survived their long imprisonment were ransomed by a French trader and sent to Quebec, and ultimately reached Plattsburg, N. Y., in the summer of 1814. Of the women, two were rescued from slavery, one by the kindness of Black Partridge; and the others doubtless perished in captivity. Of the children, we only hear again of one. In a letter written to Maj. Gen. Proctor by Capt. Bullock, the British commander at Mackinac, September 25, 1813, he says: 'There is also here a boy (Peter Bell), 5 or 6 years of age, whose father and mother were killed at Chicago. The boy was purchased from the Indians by a trader and brought here last July by direction of Mr. Dickson.' Of the six little people who fell into the hands of the Indians this one small waif alone seems to have floated to the shore of freedom.*

"The Pottawatomies, after the battle and the burning of the fort, divided their booty and prisoners and scattered, some to their villages, some to join their brethren in the siege of Fort Wayne. Here they were foiled by the timely arrival of William Henry Harrison, then Governor of the Indiana Territory, with a force of Kentucky and Ohio troops, and condign punishment was inflicted upon a part at least of the Chicago murderers. A detachment which Gen. Harrison assigned to this work was commanded by Col. Samuel Wells, who must have remembered his brother's death when he destroyed the village of Five Medals, a leading Pottawatomie chief. To one of the ruthless demons who slew women and children under the branches of this tree, such an appropriate vengeance came that it seems fitting to tell the story here. He was older than most of the band, a participant in many battles, and a deadly enemy of the whites. His scanty hair was drawn tightly upward and tied with a string, making a tuft on top of his head, and from this peculiarity he was known as Chief Shavehead. Years after the Chicago massacre he was a hunter in Western Michigan and when in liquor was fond of boasting of his achievements on the warpath. On one of these occasions in the streets of a little village he told the fearful tale of his doings on this field with all its horrors; but among his hearers chanced to be a soldier of

---

*It is due Mr. Mason to say that he had no knowledge of Mrs. Simmons and her child until after he delivered his memorial address.

the garrison of Fort Dearborn, one of the few survivors of that fatal day. As he listened he saw that frightful scene again, and was maddened by its recall. At sundown the old brave left the settlement, and silently on his trail the soldier came, 'with his gun,' says the account, 'resting in the hollow of his left arm and the right hand clasped around the lock, with his forefinger carelessly toying with the trigger.' The red man and the white passed into the shade of the forest; the soldier returned alone; Chief Shavehead was never seen again. He had paid the penalty of his crime to one who could, with some fitness, exact it. Such was the fate of a chief actor in the dark scene enacted here.

"Many others of the Pottawatomie tribe joined the British forces in the field, and at the battle of the Thames, October 5, 1813, they were confronted again by Harrison and his riflemen, who then avenged the slaughter at Chicago upon some of its perpetrators. Victor and victim alike have passed away. The story of their struggle remains, and this masterpiece will be an object-lesson teaching it to after generations. Mr. Pullman's liberal and thoughtful action is a needed recognition of the importance and interest of our early history, an inspiration to its study, and an example which may well be followed. The event which this monument commemorates, its principal incidents, and the after fortunes of those concerned in it, have been briefly sketched and much has necessarily been left unsaid. But we should not omit a grateful recognition of the able civillian soldier, William Henry Harrison, who stayed the tide of barbarism which flowed from the Chicago massacre, and humbled the tribe which was responsible for that lurid tragedy. The name of Harrison is intimately and honorably associated with the early days in the Northwest, with the war of 1812, and with the highest office in the gift of the American people half a century ago. It is likewise intimately and honorably associated with the later days of the Northwest and the great civil war, and again with the highest office in the gift of the American people in our own times. It is fitting that the distinguished descendant of William Henry Harrison should be here to-day. It is a high honor that the eminent ex-President of the United States should grace this occasion with his presence, which makes these exercises complete."

Mr. Mason having told the story of the Fort Dearborn tragedy as it deserves and as it has never before been told, it remains for this humble sketch to devote itself chiefly to the fate of the persons with whom our story especially deals.

Returning to the fort where we left the line of march forming, Corporal Simmons remained by the wagon until his duty called him away. He then lifted David, "the curly headed Corporal," in his arms and, after both father and mother had kissed him for the last time, he placed him in the government wagon, then turning to his wife who held their babe, he embraced and kissed both, then held the babe up to receive the last kiss from its little brother. Then bidding his brave and faithful wife remain close by the children in the wagon he took his place among the troops who were ordered to guard the wagons and women and children, a position in which he had requested to be placed that he might defend his family to the last. Little David with eight other children, too small to walk, occupied the government wagon as it was called. Mrs. Simmons carried her babe in her arms while Peter Bell, six years old, with seven other children were with their mothers who were on foot near the wagon, making eighteen children in all. Mrs. Heald and Mrs. Helm rode on horseback with their husbands and Capt. Wells, while Mrs. Simmons, Mrs. Bell and Mrs. Holt with four other women, whose names are unknown, were on foot near the wagon containing the children, altogether constituting a group of seven women and eighteen children.

No sooner had the train left the fort than the Indians rushed into the stockade to take possession and secure the booty abandoned and perhaps assure themselves of the treachery of Capt. Heald in destroying the arms and ammunition and also to prevent the return of any of the garrison when attacked.

No more favorable position to suit the purpose of the Indians could have been selected than that occupied by the line of march. The slender column was flanked on the left by the lake and on the right by the sand hills which were occupied by the savages and from which they suddenly poured down a shower of balls without exposing their own persons. The column was instantly halted when Capt. Wells discovered that it was surrounded by the assailants, and at the suggestion of Capt. Wells, Capt. Heald formed a line and charged up the sand hills through the line of Indians, and took a position on a mound in the prairie where they held the enemy at bay for a time. In the meanwhile, the baggage train, with the women and children remained near the lake, with the twelve militia men and a mere handful of regulars to guard them. The greater part of the soldiers who were not already killed or wounded had escaped with Capt. Heald and were now outside the

Indian lines. The savages soon discovered the almost defenceless condition of the baggage train and of the women and children, fired a volley upon them and then rushed in from front, rear and right, with uplifted tomahawks. The few soldiers having discharged their rifles and being too closely pressed to reload them, continued the unequal contest with clubbed guns until every one was slain.

It was at this time that the brave Capt. Wells returned through the Indian lines to the defense of the women and children, and dealt death among the savages until covered with wounds he fell with his face to the enemy, confronting death as a brave knight in defense of the helpless. He might have remained on the mound and surrendered with Capt. Heald and Lieut. Helm, and perhaps saved his life, but his cowardly and treacherous Miamis had betrayed him and fled to the enemy, leaving him to battle and die alone. His death was a fitting close to a heroic and honorable life and the name of Capt. William Wells will ever confer lustre on the list of American heroes.

When the attack was made Corporal John Simmons, from his position near the great cottonwood, known as the "Massacre Tree," loaded and fired as rapidly as possible, and more than one dusky warrior bit the dust at the discharge of his unerring rifle, but the contest was too unequal to continue long. When too closely pressed to load and fire his gun he clubbed it and wielded it with tremendous effect. Finally covered with wounds he fell to rise no more. The vow of the previous night had been redeemed.

FORT DEARBORN MASSACRE.

No sooner had Mrs. Simmons seen her husband fall beneath the blows of the savages surrounding him than she realized that all were at the mercy of the infuriated victors. A young Indian, tomahawk in hand, climbed into the now unguarded wagon, and in utter disregard of the tears and importunities of Mrs. Simmons and the other women, struck his bloody weapon into the heads of every child within, killing them instantly. The children unconscious of the danger which beset them had gayly enjoyed the ride from the fort until the fight began. The slaughter of these innocents was one of the most pathetic and fiendish incidents in the fearful annals of Indian warfare.

At the first fire from the Indians Mrs. Holt was wounded in the foot and was rendered unable to walk when the charge was made upon the guard protecting the women and children. The savages came on enmasse firing their guns and uttering hideous yells. The horses harnessed to the wagons became ungovernable and ran over Mrs. Holt, trampling her to death. Mrs. Bell was also severely and perhaps fatally wounded and finally tomahawked to death. Her husband, a soldier, was slain in action, leaving little Peter Bell, a boy six years old, the lone survivor of the family, a prisoner in the hands of the savages. The boy was fortunately on foot and thus escaped the doom which fell upon all within the wagon. Three children besides those in the wagon were murdered on the spot, leaving six prisoners. Of these but two drifted back to civilization, Peter Bell and the infant babe of Mrs. Simmons, which escaped the fate of her little brother and the other children by being held in the arms of her mother during the massacre.

No sooner had the savages completed the destruction of the little force guarding the baggage train, even to the last man, than most of them hastened to aid in the capture of Capt. Heald, who with his party was now surrounded by an overwhelming force, from which there was no possible escape. Realizing this, he promptly surrendered, and the little band was marched to the captured train, where all were closely guarded while the soldiers cared for their wounded and disposed of their dead, making sure that the whites should not learn the extent of their loss, which was considerable considering the disparity in numbers of the combatants. The whites, however, were all experienced backwoods riflemen and did terrible execution with weapons greatly superior to the arms of the savages, thus amply avenging their deaths before they fell. The Indians, not yet satisfied with their fiendish barbarity, now proceeded to deliberately hack and mangle to death five of the captured and disarmed soldiers in the most diabolical manner. It has been surmised that this vile deed was done to make the loss of the whites equal their own. Whether this be true or false, the act remains one of the most infamous on record. For the purpose of distressing the other prisoners, men, women and children were compelled to witness this horrible butchery. The surviving captives, as they beheld this deed, almost envied their tortured comrades as death at length came to their relief. They could reasonably anticipate a like fate, unless their heartless captors could realize more ransom money, whiskey or ammunition for their lives than for scalps, the life itself being of no value in their view. Mrs.

Simmons discovered that the delight of the savages was much enhanced by tormenting their prisoners in every conceivable manner, thus almost invariably forcing from them manifestations of pain or anger which were sweeter than music in their ears. She therefore summoned all her marvelous fortitude to prevent any expression of the anguish which was crushing her great soul. She had scarcely thus determined until her resolution was put to the most excrutiating test. The Indians collected all the murdered children and laid them in a row with their faces downward. Two burly Indians then held her by the arms and led her slowly past the children, expecting that if her boy was one of the number she would make some demonstration at the sorrowful sight. But although her tearless eyes seemed fastened upon her dead darling's flaxen curls now matted by his blood, she passed the fearful ordeal and made no sign. Not alone, nor chiefly did considerations born of pride or hatred control her in this apparently stoical indifference. True, the indignation of her pure womanhood was aroused and fixed forever against a race capable of such hellish conduct, but to save if possible the corpse of her beautiful boy from farther mutilation and her little girl from a life with these monsters, or to perish as the last resort with it, the grand heroism nerved her to bear unmoved all events, and during the entire period of her captivity, eight long months, she met all the insults and injuries of her captors with defiance, never once during that period paying them the tribute of a tear.

CHAPTER IX.

CAPTIVITY AND RANSOM.

The arms and ammunition of the fallen and prisoners were collected. The dead were stripped of everything of value, were scalped and their scalps were strung on a pole and carried on their march as trophies of the campaign. The march was then made back to the fort, where the Indians camped for the night, and feasted on the stores, while around and near the old Massacre Tree lay stark in death thirty-eight soldiers, twelve children and two women, the mangled trophies of their infernal treachery and bloodthirstiness. Never was a memorial more worthy its object, and never were noble and heroic deeds more appropriately commemorated than by the Pullman monument. Captain William Wells, Corporal John Simmons and the other soldiers who fell on that consecrated spot all deserve to have their names emblazoned on that monument as brave martyrs to the folly of their officers.

The horrors of the past and the dread of the future produced for Mrs. Simmons another sleepless night. Flushed with their success and indulging great expectations of future triumphs, the Indians were equally wakeful. In the morning the plunder was divided and the prisoners were separated, some going to the Kankakee village, some to Green Bay, and some to Michigan.

FORT DEARBORN MASSACRE. 53

After moving out of the fort it was set on fire and burned, and the line of march for the respective villages was taken up. It fell to the lot of Mrs. Simmons to go to Green Bay and her captors crossed the Chicago river on the 16th of August and started for home. The weather being warm and pleasant the hardships of the journey to Mrs. Simmons consisted mainly in being compelled to do the drudgery of the Indians, such as gathering fuel, building fires and preparing food. On the march she walked and carried her babe, the entire distance being over two hundred miles. More than a week was employed in making the journey, a terrible week to our heroine who was sufficiently acquainted with the customs of the savages to anticipate a wild scene upon arrival at their destination. Her fears were abundantly verified. Swift runners heralded the approach of the party to the members of the tribe in camp and upon the first glimpse of the returning column the women and children sallied forth to meet it. Upon the announcement of the death of their friends they commenced a fusilade of insult upon the prisoners in every conceivable manner, such as spitting in their faces, pulling their hair, kicking them and tormenting them in various other ways. They finally reached the village where the prisoners were kept under close guard during the night. In the morning the village was early astir. The young Indians especially were abroad and clamoring in a way that boded no good to the unfortunate captives. Soon, old and young, male and female, were on the open ground outside the circle of wigwams and formed a long double line reaching to the verge of the surrounding pines. The prisoners were then marched to one end of the line and each one of the soldiers was compelled to run the gauntlet receiving blows from the women and children who formed the line, and who beat them with sticks, switches and clubs. Mrs. Simmons witnessed this characteristic exhibition of savage cruelty and hoped that her sex and the infant she held in her arms would exempt her from the cruel ordeal; but to her dismay she was led in response to the universal clamor to the starting point. Looking for a moment in horror at that long line of women and children armed with implements of torture and eager to inflict punishment upon the pale-faced squaw, then glancing at the grim warriors looking on with apparent delight at the anxiety manifested by their wives and children, she almost lost heart for a moment and instantly realizing that in all the surrounding multitude there was not a heart to sympathize, not a hand to shield, before her was a long double line of savages awaiting her approach with uplifted clubs, all seeking to excel each other in wounding and bruising their victim. It was an awful moment for the poor woman but, as she had often done before in the last twelve days, when overcome with grief and almost famished with hunger, she turned her face to heaven and reposed her trust in her creator, her only source of hope and consolation, and as if inspired with superhuman strength, she wrapped the blanket about the babe that was clinging to her bosom for protection, and folding it in her strong arms to protect it from the cruel blows of the savages, she ran rapidly down the line, reaching the goal bleeding and bruised, but with the beloved object of her solicitude unharmed.

Immediately after passing the gauntlet Mrs. Simmons was astonished to receive an act of kindness for the first time since her captivity began. An elderly squaw took her kindly by the arm and led her into a wigwam, where her wounds and bruises were washed, food was given her and she was permitted to lie down and enjoy as well as she could a much needed rest. This kindness, so opportunely and unexpectedly extended was a great solace to the distressed woman. It revived her drooping faith and courage to encounter the trials yet before her. To ordinary view her situation seemed utterly desperate. She was five hundred miles from friends, the only exception being the poor savage who had befriended her at the hazard of her own safety, doubtless, and all the intervening territory swarming with murderous war parties of Indians. Bereft of the wise council and strong support of her husband, she had been taught by her bitter experiences to rely upon the All-wise and Almighty for power and guidance.

It will not be out of place to state here that the squaw who so agreeably surprised Mrs. Simmons with her kind offices remained her friend so long as they were in the same camp. Mrs. Simmons ever after spoke of her as her Indian mother, and regretted that it was not in her power to repay her for the many favors she had received from her hands. It was a matter of especial regret to her that she had forgotten her name. Could the name and history of this noble daughter of the wilderness have been preserved along with the life of Black Partridge, their good deeds would atone somewhat for the cruelties of the more vicious of their race.

After the massacre of Fort Dearborn many of the more blood-thirsty young savages of the Pottawatomie tribe hastened east to participate in the siege of Detroit and Fort Meigs, the former having surrendered to the British and Indians on the day following the capture of Fort Dearborn. Sometime in the fall of 1812 the warriors of Green Bay with their prisoners left Green Bay and marched to the ruins of Fort Dearborn, thence around the end of lake Michigan and up to Mackinac, which was still in the hands of the British and Indians. It was winter when they reached Mackinac, and negotiations for the ransom of the prisoners were opened. Mrs. Simmons and her babe had suffered terribly while on the journey to Mackinac. Winter had come on and found her thinly clad, while she was often compelled to seek food from under the snow. Still, amid all her privations and hardships the heroic woman thought only of the safety and comfort of her child. While in Green Bay the Indians had, by various devices, attempted to take her babe from her, under the pretext of friendship. They declared they would relieve her from the burden of its care and would rear it as one of their own children. These repeated offers and their unconditional refusal led the mother to more closely watch over the babe, never permitting her to pass beyond her reach.

After many refusals a chief seized the child by the arm and attempted to drag it from its mother's breast, at the same time brandishing his tomahawk over her head with violent contortions and gesticulations, and threatening to kill her instantly unless she resigned the infant. With a look of disdain and defiance, she replied to his ferocious demonstrations that he might slay her, but separate her and her child, never! The chief finding her spirit unbroken and undismayed, relaxed his hold upon the child, and kindly though firmly said to Mrs. Simmons: "Good squaw; heap brave; may keep papoose." This was the last effort made to take her babe from her, though she maintained a vigilant watch upon it while she remained a prisoner. Neither was she farther molested in caring for it, save that the Indians compelled her to bathe it daily, for the purpose, as they said, of washing the white blood out of its veins.

At Mackinac Mrs. Simmons was much encouraged by the hope of ransom or exchange, and in order to accomplish release on some terms she was sent in midwinter from Mackinac to Detroit, a distance of over three hundred miles. Deep snows with occasional storms and blizzards impeded their march, which was on foot through a trackless wilderness. But for the knowledge Mrs. Simmons possessed that an effort was being made by government authorities to ransom her and her child and that every step she now took led her nearer liberty and friends she must have sat down in despair. Who can imagine the hidden power which sustained the poor woman as she trudged along from day to day on that long and dreary journey? Her clothing was woefully insufficient and in tatters, the weather was unendurable, and food so scarce that she often appeased hunger by eating roots, acorns and nuts found under the snow. Her babe, now a year old, had much increased in weight, yet with her own diminished strength she was obliged to carry it in her arms continually while she performed the camp drudgery for the Indians.

In the latter part of winter, when Mrs. Simmons with her captors reached Detroit they found that post in possession of the British and Indians, the latter having practical control. A large number of prisoners were captured by these allies at Frenchtown on the river Raisin in January, after a severe battle. Shortly after, Gen. Proctor, the British general, left for Malden, across the Detroit river, when the Indians butchered part of the prisoners in cold blood. The wounded had been collected in two houses: these were set on fire, and when such of the prisoners as could move attempted to leave the burning buildings they were pushed back into the flames by the savages and perished there. The few who were not butchered or burned to death, were marched as slaves to Detroit and, dragged through the streets, exposed to sale as such. The citizens sacrificed everything they could spare to ransom them from this pitiful fate. Here Mrs. Simmons saw and recognized the savage Pottawatomies, and learned with horror of their barbarities at Frenchtown, and that the entire northwest was in possession of the Indians. She had fondly hoped that her perils would end when she reached Detroit, and expected that safety which it is the boast of England prevails beneath the British flag, but soon realized that the English officers had little disposition to restrain the cruelty of the Indians. From Detroit she was taken to Fort Meigs, and on the journey witnessed the destruction effected by the savages. Late in March she arrived at Fort Meigs; which was in command of Gen. Harrison, who was laboring day and night to strengthen the fortification against the expected attack from the British and

Indians. Here Mrs. Simmons was set at liberty among friends and joyfully learned that a supply train had just arrived from Cincinnati, and would immediately return under a strong escort. The train was to pass on return within a few miles of her home in Miami county, Ohio. She was still two hundred miles from home, the streams were swollen, the swamps covered with water, the roads deep in mud and slush, and the weather chilly, all combined making the journey disagreeable. But Mrs. Simmons contrasted it with her recent experience, and decided that after traveling nearly 400 miles, from Mackinac to Fort Meigs, through fierce storms and bitter cold, poorly clad, almost starved, bearing night and day the growing burden of her child, a slave to savage brutes, and forced to plod every step of the long way on feet almost bare, swollen and bleeding, the present trip was a delightful pleasure excursion. She was now among friends, with no great apprehension of danger from enemies, warmly wrapped in blankets and sheltered in a comfortable government wagon, enjoying plenty of civilized food, and conscious that each day's march brought her nearer her longed for destination.

On a day about the middle of April, 1813, the train passed four miles south of her home. Here she left the wagons and escort with many heart-felt thanks for the kindness shown her on the march, and taking her babe in her arms walked swiftly along a dim path through the forest. The country was infested with predatory scalping bands of Indians, ready to pounce upon defenseless travelers or isolated settlers for plunder or revenge. But the thoughts of the lone woman were busy with retrospect of the eventful past, rather than with forebodings of the future. Every step was bringing her nearer the home which she had left two years before in company with her young soldier husband and their first born, little David. During the short journey to the dear home what pictures rose before her mental vision. The march of the little family through the woods, the rumbling of the coming storm, the heart-sickening details of the evacuation and the massacre of the soldiers, death of her brave husband, the slaughter of the innocents, David among them, the awful death of the captured soldiers, the fearful gauntlet, the exhausting marches through extreme cold, blinding storms and freezing mud and water, the miseries of starvation, and if it were possible to represent it, over all and through all the anxiety which knew neither palliation or cessation. As her heart burned within her at the remembrance of these experiences she found herself at the door of the blockhouse. To the inmates she appeared as one risen from the dead, for they had long before resigned themselves to the belief that the entire family of their son had fallen. The mutual, mingled feelings of grief, joy, thankfulness and sympathy, may well be left to the imagination of our readers without attempted description. It was long before the terrible tidings became an old story in recital, and as for the narrator herself, her long repressed emotions were so completely broken down by the return that to use her own language, she "did nothing but weep for months."

CHAPTER X.

THE MASSACRE OF NEIGHBORS, HER ONLY SISTER AMONG THEM.

Arrived at home Mrs. Simmons hoped that her trials were over, but she was soon to be terribly undeceived. Her only sister married a Henry Dilbone in Lancaster county, Pa., and they emigrated to Ohio in 1807, settling near the Simmons blockhouse where they opened a small farm. Here in the summer of 1813 they were living happily with their family of small children. Occasionally an alarm of Indian raids caused them to take temporary shelter in the blockhouse. The situation in the northwest was truly gloomy. The barbarities of the Indians and their British allies at Mackinac, Dearborn, Detroit, Frenchtown, the river Raisin, and Fort Meigs, where prisoners fell into their hands had brought mourning to almost every family. Many women and children had been carried away into slavery. So far the savages had been successful in almost every engagement. They were therefore frenzied with daring and cruelty. It had become a war of extermination on both sides, and the lives of friendly Indians were often sacrificed by the enraged frontiersmen in retaliation for crimes committed by the hostiles. Many camps of peaceable savages existed all through the settlements, and their inmates were compelled to endure many hardships as it was not safe for them to go abroad to hunt or seek food.

At this time there was an Indian camp at Piqua on the Miami river, and others in the vicinity. About the middle of August, 1813, three or four Indians in a canoe dropped down the river to near the mouth of Spring creek, where they were seen late in the evening by Dr. Coleman, of Troy, and from this action were supposed to be a fishing party. On the following day, about four o'clock in the afternoon they fired on and killed David Gerard, near his residence, about two miles north of the mouth of Spring creek. Having secured his scalp they fled north about four miles to the Dilbone farm. Henry Dilbone and his family were at some distance from the house in a field, which was surrounded by woods on three sides, engaged in pulling flax, from which to make clothing for the household. Adjoining the flax patch was a small field of corn within which an Indian had secreted himself, waiting an opportunity to slay the entire family. The sinking sun casting its lurid glare on the surrounding forest, and the evening shades fast settling down upon that sultry August day, warned the tired laborers that their day's work was nearly completed. Little did they dream how near the end of their earthly toil approached. Their faithful dog discovered the savage lying in wait, gave the alarm and almost simultaneously with his loud bark a gun was discharged, Mr. Dilbone receiving a ball from the rifle of the Indian in his breast. The assassin at the same instant sprang from his place of concealment and rushed forward to tomakawk and scalp his victim, but Mr. Dilbone as quickly recovered from the shock and ran rapidly south, leaping over the fence into the thick brush bordering a swamp where he fell. The savage abandoned the pursuit of Mr. Dilbone, perhaps not aware of the severity of his wound, being deceived by his speed, now turned his attention to Mrs. Dilbone, who at a glance saw the situation and fled into the corn on the west for concealment, but was overtaken by the fiendish savage. A single blow from his tomahawk felled her to the earth, where, after taking her scalp, he left her weltering in her blood.

During the time in which this terrible tragedy was being enacted, the four little children were horrified witnesses, and momentarily expected the same fate. The eldest son, John, being less than ten years of age, took his little brother, now in his seventh month, in his arms and set out for the house, but being encumbered with the babe and his little sisters who were but three and four years old, made slow progress over the rough ground. They had gotten but a little way when the fiend left his other victims and started toward them. But to the report of his own gun, the continued barking of the dog and the screams of Mrs. Dilbone, was now added the report of another fire arm a short distance away, which so alarmed the Indian that he instantly fled into the the deep forest leaving his rifle and blanket where he had dropped them in pursuit of his victims. He then, as stated in the History of Ohio, "hastened north to receive the bounty for his scalps from the British authorities." More probably, from the agents of the British Hudson Bay Company. The fact that the savage fled without his gun is evidence that he was terribly alarmed, and this belief in his imminent peril was the salvation of the helpless children. The neighbors were speedily alarmed and collecting at once went in quest of Mr. and Mrs. Dilbone, accompanied by the eldest son as a guide. The dead body of Mrs. Dilbone was found which, with the children, was taken to the Simmons blockhouse for safety. In ignorance of the number of the assailants and fearing an ambuscade, darkness having already settled upon the dense forest, farther search for Mr. Dilbone was postponed until the following morning when a company of militia, under Capt. Wm. McKinney, which had rallied at the Simmons blockhouse during the night, started with the rising sun in search of the wounded man. In searching the neighboring woods the company passed so near him that he saw and heard them. As the rear soldier, Jacob Simmons, was passing by where he lay, Mr. Dilbone cried out in the accents of despair, "For God's sake, don't all pass me again!" The poor man lay just where he had first fallen, so exhausted that he was unable to rise or make any outcry audible to his son and the party which on the previous evening removed the body of his wife, and whom he heard distinctly. All night he had lain between two oaks, one of which has been spared by time and the woodman and still stands, a living monument to the memory of Henry Dilbone. How little can the men of this generation realize the dreadful anguish under that veteran oak during that awful August night. Uncertainty regarding the fate of his loved and helpless family prompted him to rise and drag himself to them. Failing utterly in this attempt, he strove to staunch the streaming wound in his bosom. Tortured with the agony of pain and consuming thirst, he could only lie helpless and well nigh hopeless and wait for the morning. Beside such anguish of body and mind how trivial seem many of our loudly lamented calamities.

The almost unconscious man was borne to the block house, and a messenger was sent to summon the distinguished Dr. Coleman from Troy—the only surgeon then residing in Miami county, who came and attended the dying sufferer until the following day when he expired in the presence of his children.

It was a sad coincidence when the dead and mangled body of the only sister of Mrs. Simmons was brought to the Simmons homestead on the first anniversary of the murder of her husband and son and her own capture. Surely her vivid remembrance of the events of the massacre and consequent captivity had been sufficiently bitter without this final draught of the cup of sorrow on the first recurrence of the black day. Mrs. Simmons and the other inmates of the blockhouse had been informed by a runner of the hellish deed and awaited the coming of the mournful procession which bore the mortal remains of her beloved sister accompanied by her four small orphan children. Another coincidence connecting this transaction with her own sad story which profoundly impressed Mrs. Simmons was the fact of the babe in its seventh month being bereft of its parents as her own infant had been robbed of its father a year before at the same tender age. That night of sorrow was a painful vigil for Mrs. Simmons. Her only sister, beloved as a cherished companion for almost a life time, lay a bloody corpse in the house. The cries of bereaved children, her own thoughts mingling ghastly memories with well-founded forebodings of future outrages from the savages believed to be prowling in the neighborhood, together with the agonizing uncertainty regarding the fate of her wounded brother-in-law, all combined to render the watch of the terribly tried woman the extremity. of mental torture.

Mr. and Mrs. Dilbone were buried near where they fell, a few feet north of the section line, five miles east of Piqua on the turnpike and old military road over which a stream of emigrants have passed for more than eighty years, unconscious that they trod upon the unmarked graves of these martyrs to civilization.

CHAPTER XI.

AT REST

During the years of peace and rural plenty which followed the eventful era of exploration and conquest the infant child of Mrs. Simmons, whose life morning opened so wild and ominous, grew to womanhood and became a happy wife and mother. Her husband, Moses Winans, settled in Shelby county, Ohio, when her aged mother took up her residence in her daughter's family. In 1853, Mrs. Simmons removed with the Winans family to Springville, Linn county, Iowa, where she died, February 27th, 1857, at the mature age of eighty years.

The friends of Mrs. Simmons applied for and secured a pension for her, but she only received one payment, the pitiful sum of thirty dollars. The reason for the suspension of this payment was never known to her.

In all the annals of the race no grander exhibition of courage, devotion and fortitude can be found. No Spartan mother could have more effectually fortified her feelings against expression, when the slightest manifestation of weakness had been fatal. Upon this lone woman culminated all the horrors which the most ingenious tortures could devise, while she endured so well the extremity of mental anguish, yet these almost incredible sufferings could not force from her proud, heroic spirit the tribute of a solitary tear to her tormentors. She passed the awful ordeal unscathed from dishonor or weakness and is entitled to a leading place among American Heroines.

A few words may be properly devoted at this place to a character previously introduced and well worthy mention on account of his exemplary and useful life. Tom Rodgers passed the three years of the war in the woods scouting and watching the movements of the Indians. He slept in the houses of settlers only in very cold weather. After the war he built for himself a small cabin in the forest on the banks of Spring Creek, in the vicinity of which he spent his life alone, hunting to supply himself with food and clothing, until about 1850, when he became feeble from age and was taken to the county asylum, near Troy, where he died a year or two later. The service which he rendered during the war so endeared Tom Rodgers to the settlers that he was at all times a welcome guest, but he very seldom took advantage of their generosity, preferring the life of a hermit. He lived more than the allotted three score years and ten- -a life which experienced the marvelous transition from the unbroken solitudes of a trackless wilderness to the perfect civilization of a mighty commonwealth.

CHAPTER XII.

AWAITING THE END.

Mrs. Winans has unquestionably for many years been the sole survivor of the Fort Dearborn massacre. Certainly for more than thirty years has this claim been true. It is also almost certain that she was the only person born there who escaped death on that fatal day, Peter Bell being the only competitor for this distinction with the weight of evidence in her favor.

In the number of the "Illustrated Pacific States" for June, 1893, the following article with an excellent cut of the subject appears, contributed by Mrs. Florence M. Kimball.

"It is interesting to know that there is now living the first white child born in the famous city by the lakes. Mrs. Susan Winans of Santa Ana, Orange county, California, enjoys this distinction. When old Fort Dearborn was standing on the site of one of the greatest cities on the American continent, and savage Indians held supreme sway, Susan Simmons first saw the light in that historic fort.

"Her father, John Simmons, a Pennsylvanian by birth, married Miss Susan Millhouse, also a Pennsylvanian. He enlisted in the war of 1812, and was sent to the frontier, Fort Dearborn. While on a furlough he visited his young wife and persuaded her to return with him, taking with them their little two-year old son, David. On February 13th, 1812, Susan was born. The discomforts and trials of the young mother, surrounded by hostile Indians, and the life of her husband constantly endangered, can never be told. Her devotion to her family and wonderful heroism sustained her; even when in the following August her husband and little son were killed at the terrible Indian massacre, and she, with her infant, Susan, were taken prisoners, she still maintained her courageous bearing. In April of the next year an exchange was effected, and the bereaved mother and little daughter returned to the parental roof in Ohio. In 1828 Susan Simmons was married to Mr. M. P. Winans. Nine children were born to them, six of whom are living, three in Orange county, Cal., and three in Iowa, to which state Mr. and Mrs. Winans moved in 1853. Born in the midst of dangers, her life has been one of heroic acts, noble sacrifices and gentle, womanly deeds of love and kindness. Although eighty-three years of age, she might easily be taken for sixty; her handwriting is that of a much younger person, and all her faculties are unimpaired. Enveloped in the domestic sunshine of her daughter's happy home, Grandma Winans' declining years are made bright and pleasant by its members. The children of the neighborhood love her as if she were their own. I visited her on May Day and found the vine-embowered cottage porch gay with May baskets left by the little ones, with the message, "For Grandma."

"Anxious that Mrs. Winans should be represented either in the Woman's building at Chicago, or the reconstructed Fort Dearborn, I have made partial arrangement for a life-size crayon portrait to be made by her granddaughter, who is a fine artist. Mrs. Potter Palmer has asked for the glass of jelly made by her, and placed by the citizens of Santa Ana on a handsome silver stand, for the Woman's building. In reply to the question if she would not like to visit the Exposition, she replied, with a smile of satisfaction: 'Oh, no; I have lived in the delightful climate of Southern California too long to be willing to encounter the storms of the East.' "

"Such, in brief," concludes an article in the San Francisco *Evening Chronicle* of corresponding date with the issue of the *Illustrated Pacific States*, "is the life history of the first white child born in Chicago." And this humble sketch may fittingly conclude in the graphic language of another review of this eventful life:

"In winterless California one of the most notable vestiges of the formative life of the nation abides in peace and quiet the inevitable change. Into her infant ears dinned the reveille of camp and the war hoop of the savage; her innocent eyes beheld father and brother fall in awful death. At a mother's breast she clung close that no club might bruise her tender frame. From that terrible dream of destruction and death to the vast Chicago, hostess of the nations in her peerless palaces by the illuminated lake, from the awful glare of the burning fort upon its unburied victims to the dazzling lights of Fairyland, from the temporary triumph of savagery to the eternal victory of the arts of civilization spans the extent of this phenomenal life."

CHAPTER XIII.

THE POTTAWATOMIE TRIBE.

To perfect this narrative a brief history of the Pottawatomie Indians is essential. They are of Algonquin stock, crafty and hardy, possessing strong passions and as enemies are fierce and relentless. The establishment of Fort Dearborn in the center of their territory in 1803 excited their jealousy. Gen. Harmer had penetrated to the border of their domain and laid the country waste in the fall of 1790. In November, 1791, Gen. St. Clair had reached the vicinity of the Indian villages for the purpose of destroying them. In 1794 General Wayne killed many of their warriors and laid the country waste early in the fall. In November, 1811, Gen. Harrison defeated the Indians at Tippecanoe and destroyed the village with the food provided for the winter. These campaigns, although not uniformly successful, entailed great hardships upon the Indians. The destruction of their winter supplies at the approach of cold weather was exceedingly exasperating. These events recalled to their minds by the firey eloquence of Tecumseh became more provocation for war at each fresh recital. The Pottawatomies had long waited for the opportunity which now presented itself to seek revenge for these wrongs and to drive the Americans from their territory. The remembrance of the excesses perpetrated by vicious whites upon peaceable Indians added to the natural resentment of the fierce tribes. It is therefore not to be deemed surprising in view of the peculiarities of Indian character that the atrocities of Dearborn, Frenchtown, Meigs and Detroit should have been committed.

We have written the bloody record of the Pottawatomies as we found it, but desiring to do the tribe justice, we note with pleasure the good deeds of Black Partridge and the noble Indian mother to whose care and kindness Mrs. Simmons probably owed her life and the life of her child, and through the efforts of the chief her restoration to her friends. Black Partridge deserves more than a passing notice for his timely warning to the doomed garrison and his heroic efforts to save the lives of the whites on the battle field at the hazard of his own. His identity concealed beneath war paint, he was liable to be shot down by those whom he endeavored to save. There may have been others as noble as those we have mentioned whose names will forever remain buried in oblivion. Later in the history of Chicago and northern Illinois, Chief Shabbona was prominent as an advocate for peace. He stood by the side of Tecumseh when that warrior fell, and soon after became the fast friend of the whites and devoted the remainder of his life to sincere efforts to maintain peace between the settlers and Indians, and between the several tribes. Pokanoka, squaw of Chief Shabbona, faithfully seconded him in his labor of love and mercy. The lives of many of the earlier settlers were saved by the timely warning given them by these noble missionaries of mercy.

There are a few Pottawatomies in Michigan, a few in Nebraska, Wisconsin and the Indian territory, but the majority of the tribe, consisting of the Prairie Band, reside on their reservation in Jackson county, Kansas. This reservntion is twelve miles square. They pay no taxes and maintain their tribal relation. The United States government sustains a very extensive boarding school here. During the last quarter of 1895 eighty-nine boys and fifty-four girls from the Pottawatomie tribe also attended Haskell Institute, an Indian Training School maintained at Lawrence, Kansas, by the general government. A school is also in operation in Nebraska for the benefit of the Pottawatomies. They have now standing to their credit on the books of the Interior Department at Washington a total of $635,816.28. Thus whatever were the provocations furnished by the whites to inspire the cruelties of the Pottawatomies in the remote past, it is obvious that the surviving members of the tribe are in receipt of especial favors from the pale faces of the present time. These figures also contrast with the pitiful sums paid by the same government to the brave men who left homes and families exposed to the assaults of the merciless savages and from whose sacrifices and sufferings sprang the mighty empire of the northwest. While the descendants of the butchers of Fort Dearborn are lavishly provided for by the government, it is not too much to expect that the memories of the men and women who planted the outposts of civilization and defended them with their blood and lives shall be held in everlasting remembrance by the millions who shall occupy the fair heritage these heroic pioneers won from the wilderness.

The tribe touches by one link the period of the massacre. The present chief, Shaugh-nes-see, was born on the Kankakee in 1812. His grandfather, Suna-we-wone, was in command of the Pottawatomies at the Fort Dearborn fight. His father, Wab-sai was also a participant in the slaughter of the garrison. Shaugh-nessee lives on the tribal reservation in Jackson county, Kansas. In a recent interview with him, he stated in reply to questions that the evening before the battle a white man (meaning probably Capt. Wells) who had been raised by Indians rode into the stockade, and that he tried to escape the next day but was killed by the savages. Also that a party of soldiers escaped to a mound but were captured and killed. To the question as to the number and disposition of prisoners taken, he believed that no captives were taken, the entire garrison having been slain. He had understood that the treachery of the officers in destroying the stores of the fort was one of the main causes of the massacre. All these statements were of course founded upon the traditions of the tribe often repeated in the hearing of the chief, and furnished an illustration of the reliability of such evidence as the sole support of history.

N. SIMMONS, M. D.

Proprietor of Simmons Liver Tablets or Ginger Snaps.

The following extract is from the Select Friend the organ of the order of that name:

"The Doctor has been one of the leading Physicians of Lawrence for many years. He is also one of our most reliable citizens. He has been a member of the Legislature; Mayor of our city; member of the State Board of Health, Coroner; County Health Officer; President and Secretary successively of the State Medical Association, etc.; and has always acquitted himself with credit in whatever position he has been called. His Tablets were first made to use in his practice but soon, by reason of their intrinsic merit, acquired a local reputation, and for several years their use has been gradually extended until now their manufacture and sale has become a business of considerable magnitude. We know of families who would not think of keeping house without them."

THE HUMAN SYSTEM.

By the harmonious action of this mechanism it is constantly renewing itself. Worn, effete material is eliminated by the excretory organs, while fresh supplies are prepared and assimilated to take its place. If the equilibrum between these functions is disturbed, and elimination proceeds rapidly, while assimilation is suspended, the system becomes emaciated and blood impoverished, resulting in anemia, vertigo, neuralgia, cramps, nervous headache indigestion, constipation, paresis, paralysis, palpitation, irregular action of the liver, kidneys, skin, brain and heart, with horrid mental forebodings and fleeting pains in all parts of the body.

To attempt to correct this condition with active cathartics, only increases the danger, by hastening excretion and farther impairing assimilation. To attempt this correction with opiate or alcoholic narcotics is equally fallacious, for while excretion is delayed, assimilation is also impaired, and life endangered by the retention of the morbid material. On the other hand, if excretion is retarded and assimilation active, perversion of the blood follows. The process of the renewal of life is arrested, colonies of microbes find lodgment in the accumulated detritus which clog the free circulation of the blood, resulting in congestion, tuberculosis, scroffula, eczema, tumors, cancers, consumption, epilepsy, paralysis, apoplexy, rheumatism, gout, dropsy and Bright's disease, with blood poison and physical degeneration of the brain, lungs, heart, liver, stomach and kidneys.

The proper remedies to employ are those that vitalize all of the functions of the system, and restore lost action of the stomach and bowels, strengthen and energize the brain and nervous system, stimulate the liver and kidneys, and give force to the heart and circulaton of the blood, thereby relieving congestion and preventing the development of the many dangerous diseases above enumerated before organic disintegration has proeeded too far to admit of recovery.

There is no household remedy on the market that is equal to

SIMMONS LIVER TABLETS OR GINGER SNAPS

to correct these morbid functional processes and restore normal action. They are so accurately compounded that while they hasten the removal of waste, they stimulate assimilation and maintain harmony in the organism which is indispensible to health.

ORIGIN OF THE NAME.

THE UNIQUE NAME OF
SIMMONS LIVER TABLETS OR GINGER SNAPS.

Did not originate in an eccentric freak of the proprietor. They were widely known by this name many years before printed labels or circulars were prepared and could not well be changed without causing unavoidable confusion.

HOW TO DO GOOD.

Call on your neighbor who has sick headache and often complains of constipation, biliousness, torpid liver, weak stomach and is generally miserable and don't let him or her rest until made happy by the exhilerating effects of **Simmons Liver Tablets or Ginger Snaps.**

NOTICE.

It is due the public to say that Simmons Liver Tablets or Ginger Snaps will not cure all organic diseases in their advanced stage; notably cancers and consumption, but their timely use will prevent organic disintegration by arresting the morbid processes leading to their destruction.

They keep the Life Renewing Mechanism Running.

If the dotage of age or decline is creeping upon you take Simmons Liver Tablets or Ginger Snaps and stimulate the renewal of life and you will be surprised at the happy results, that aged and haggard look and feeling due to general debility will be replaced by youthful freshness and vivacity.

A HINT.

Persons who use Simmons Liver Tablets or Ginger Snaps seldom have to call in a physician.

To the Despondent.

Do not abandon hope while you can purchase 200 doses of Simmons Liver Tablets or Ginger Snaps for $1.00 and remove the physical condition which makes you melancholy and miserable.

READ THE FOLLOWING SPECIAL DIRECTIONS.

For Constipation:—Take 1 to 6 tablets, or as many as may be required 3 times a day until action is established. Then enough daily at bed time to produce a free operation on the following morning.

For Sick Headache, Vertigo and Dizziness:—Take the same as for Constipation and it will only be a question of time when you will be free from your tormentor.

For Indigestion, (Dyspepsia):—Take as many as the bowels will bear immediately before or after each meal.

Congestion or Inflamed Liver:—Symptoms; fulness, pain and soreness at the lower edge of the ribs on the right side.

Take 1 to 4 tablets every 3 hours until free action is established; then repeat from 1 to 3 times a day as long as required.

Weakness of the Kidneys and Bladder:—Elderly persons, especially who are much disturbed of their rest at night will be greatly relieved by taking as many as the bowels will bear at early bed time.

For Old Age:—Use freely and postpone its ravages.

Threatened Paralysis and Apoplexy:—Symptoms; numbness, tingling in the extremities, pain and dizziness in the head, weakness, unsteady gait and loss of memory. Take as many as the bowels will bear from 1 to 3 times a day.

For Heart Failure, Weakness:—Take as many as the bowels will bear 2 or 3 times a day as a tonic to the pneumogastric nerve and muscles of the heart.

In all Fevers:—Take enough daily to keep the bowels in good condition.

For Diarrhœa:—Take a tablet every 2 hours until the discharges are corrected then 2 or 3 times a day. If chronic take 1 from 1 to 3 times a day.

For Dysentary:—Take 2 to 5 tablets every 3 hours until natural stools are produced; then repeat 3 times a day.

Explanation:—As many as the bowels will bear means not to exceed two or three operations daily.

Containing no mercury, Simmons Liver Tablets or Ginger Snaps may be taken by persons of all ages and conditions for an indefinate period without injury. Children must take less in proportion to age.

Call for Simmons Liver Tablets or Ginger Snaps and refuse all substitutes as there is no similar remedy on the market that can be safely employed in their stead.

For Sale by all Druggists, or sent by Mail on receipt of Price.

A SINGLE BOX FOR 25 CENTS.

Five Boxes for $1.00.

ADDRESS,

N. SIMMONS, M. D.,
Lawrence, Kansas.

www.ingramcontent.com/pod-product-compliance
Lightning Source LLC
Chambersburg PA
CBHW031608110426
42742CB00037B/1330